Getti
Work

Mary Coussey

The Chartered Institute of Personnel and Development is the leading publisher of books and reports for personnel and training professionals, students, and all those concerned with the effective management and development of people at work. For full details of all our titles, please contact the Publishing Department:

Tel: 020 8263 3387
Fax: 020 8263 3850

E-mail: publish@cipd.co.uk

The catalogue of all CIPD titles can be viewed on the CIPD website:
www.cipd.co.uk/publications

Getting the Right Work–Life Balance

Implementing family-friendly practices

Mary Coussey

**Judge Institute of Management Studies,
University of Cambridge**

First published 2000

Cover design by Curve
Designed and typeset by Beacon GDT
Printed in Great Britain by Short Run Press

British Library Cataloguing in Publication Data
A catalogue record for this book is available from the British Library

ISBN 0 85292 895 5

Chartered Institute of Personnel and Development,
CIPD House, Camp Road, London SW19 4UX

Tel: 020 8971 9000
Fax: 020 8263 3333
Website: www.cipd.co.uk

Incorporated by Royal Charter. Registered charity no. 1079797.

Contents

Acknowledgements

The author wishes to thank the companies that took part in this study for their help and for giving up their time. She also wishes to thank the members of the research project steering group, who gave valuable ideas, contacts and support.

Foreword

Time is the enemy: work intensity and long hours are the twin downsides of today's labour market. Legislation on working time has focused attention on the problem without offering any reliable formula for tackling it. People are clamouring for a better work–life balance. They are also looking for practical guidance on how to achieve it.

This report focuses on how 12 organisations – large, medium and small – have sought to give employees more flexibility in the hours they work. The study was undertaken on the initiative of the CIPD Mid and North Anglia branch, and all the employers studied are located in that area. There is already substantial evidence about the business benefits of adopting so-called 'family-friendly' practices: a number of studies underline the links with employee satisfaction, as well as the labour market factors that have encouraged employers to think harder about how to recruit and retain good people. But the same studies also show that relatively few employers have adopted such practices. What are the factors that have influenced those employers that have adopted them, and what difficulties have they encountered? These are the basic questions the present study was designed to answer.

Unsurprisingly, many employers who participated in the study said they had been influenced by difficulties in recruiting and retaining experienced employees, particularly those in senior professional and technical jobs. Some, however, had business philosophies underpinning their concern to offer employees more flexibility, including a commitment to maintaining a positive 'psychological contract' with employees and building a good reputation with both staff and customers. Clearly such employers have a vision of competitive success that is linked to practising consistent values and behaviour and goes beyond the measurement of short-term costs and benefits.

Two findings in particular stand out as somewhat unexpected. One is the importance of employee demand as an influence on employer practice. The main reason why many of these organisations adopted family-friendly practices was often simply that employees asked for them. This is particularly the case with access to part-time employment, which seems in practice to be the most important way in which many employers seek to offer employees flexibility within the employment contract. This suggests that more employers could be persuaded to change existing practices where employees are willing to communicate their wish for greater flexibility.

A second unexpected finding is the limited impact that either legislation or trade unions appear to have had on employers' practices. This may possibly be a product of the particular sample and it is unclear why more impact was not identified, particularly in organisations where trade unions were recognised. This may be an area in which further research would be helpful.

The main constraint on the wider adoption of such practices seems to have been managers' beliefs about the problems of accommodating flexibility with operational and business needs. In practice many managers continue to believe that family-friendly practices 'couldn't work here', for a variety of technical, practical, cultural or other reasons. No doubt in some cases these concerns are well founded, but in others they are more about a lack of familiarity or flexible thinking. The positive comments by managers about part-time employees – for example 'very dedicated and loyal', 'they are not clock-watchers' – help to demonstrate what managers have to gain.

This surely demonstrates the key role personnel managers can play in influencing other managers and selling the benefits of family-friendly practices. This is where the adoption of policy statements can help in getting the ball rolling, underlining senior management commitment and marshalling the business arguments. As the report concludes, the issues are largely about good communication, and language can be important. Some employees reportedly object to 'family-friendly' practices because they can discriminate against those without families. By focusing on flexibility and work–life balance, employers can deal with this argument and make clear that the benefits of flexibility apply to men and women, married and single people, younger and older workers, those with children and those without. This is an issue that reinforces the case for diversity.

The CIPD commends this report to all those looking for practical ways of bringing practice more closely into line with rhetoric in this area, so enhancing both employee satisfaction and business performance.

Mike Emmott

Chartered Institute of Personnel and Development

Executive summary

- The report presents the findings of a study that was commissioned by the Mid and North Anglia Branch of the CIPD. The study looked at the practical implications of family-friendly working practices in 12 organisations, representing a diverse group of small, medium and large Mid and North Anglian industries, including the growing knowledge-based high technology sectors, manufacturing and food. The aim was to review the practical arrangements, the business benefits found, any costs and constraints, take-up and the attitudes of employees and managers.

- In the last 15 years there has been a large increase in flexible working, both in response to market pressure and to meet employees' needs to balance work and family life. The Government has recently published guidance to encourage businesses to introduce practices to help employees balance work and the rest of life, and CIPD research shows that work–life balance is a key factor in establishing a positive psychological contract.

- There has been considerable research in order to help define flexible working and family-friendly policies, including policies concerned with hours of work, leave entitlement and assistance with family responsibilities. Research has also covered the scale and extent of family-friendly policies, take-up, the business benefits and obstacles to family-friendly work, and the position of small employers. The study used the research findings as a basis for examining the practical questions involved in the participating organisations. There is a wide variety of practices included in the case studies, but the focus in interviews was often on flexible. working practices such as part-time jobs and self-employment, which were seen as the most significant adjustments being made to meet employees' needs for work–life balance.

- There were a variety of reasons given for the introduction of family-friendly practices. Most case study organisations gave the need to retain skilled staff, particularly women with young children, as the principal reason for introducing flexible arrangements such as part-time working. Other reasons given were the need to meet operational requirements and the desire to be seen as a good employer. Recent legislation had caused the participants to review their leave entitlements, but leave was less important for retaining employees than the introduction of flexible working arrangements. In many cases, part-time and other flexible working practices were introduced informally in response to employee requests rather than as a result of a formal policy.

- The case study organisations reported significant business benefits from implementing family-friendly policies. These benefits were found equally in the small and medium-sized firms in the study. The benefits included higher productivity by employees who worked part-time and other non-standard arrangements. For example, some did a full-time job in three or four days. The employers also reported increased flexibility from employing several part-timers, who could provide cover for absenteeism and holidays, and offer cover for longer hours, thus providing better customer service. Another reported advantage was that people whose work–life balance needs had been met were highly motivated and committed to the company. They were felt to be more reliable and dedicated than many full-time staff. Specific provisions, such as a holiday playscheme and a childcare subsidy, were found to be a bonus in recruitment and to improve retention.

◘ Although employers reported some additional costs from employing part-timers, such as extra co-ordination and training, these were felt to be outweighed by the gains. The greatest difficulty reported was in persuading managers to accept more flexible working arrangements, although once they experienced the benefits, managers became strong advocates of flexibility.

◘ Employees who were interviewed provided clear evidence of the business benefits of family-friendly arrangements. They were determined to put in extra effort and be highly productive; they were flexible and were committed to their employers because their needs had been recognised. They reported being less likely to be away for sickness and domestic reasons, and were less likely to leave. Managers too were very positive about their experience of flexible working. They found that part-time staff gave additional flexibility, higher productivity, additional cover and they were able to reduce costs because they used fewer temporary staff.

◘ Most HR managers were expecting an increase in the numbers of staff who work non-standard hours. This was partly because of demographic trends, including increased participation at work both by women with families, and of older employees, in consequence of the 'ageing' population. These people would want flexible working arrangements. It was also reported that changing social attitudes were making it more important for employers to meet employees' needs for work–life balance.

◘ The studies suggest that there is a need to formalise flexible working practices into specific policies and criteria, to help ensure that there is consistency between departments and to make it easier for employees to take advantage of the opportunities without feeling that they have to negotiate. Guidance on the practical arrangements, such as how to divide jobs and ensure co-ordination and good communications within the organisation and with clients, helps dispel assumptions about the difficulties of implementing family-friendly practices. This may help to encourage the take-up of family-friendly arrangements.

◘ Take-up may also be easier if employers foster a culture in which family-friendly arrangements are part of accepted practice. This includes disseminating information about the success of existing methods, and reviewing the scope for greater flexibility. These steps can help reduce assumptions that family-friendly practices could not be offered in certain departments.

1 | Background to the study

◘ **In the last 15 years, there has been a large increase in flexible working, both in response to market pressure and to meet employees' needs.**

◘ **CIPD research shows that work–life balance is a key factor in establishing a positive psychological contract.**

◘ **There has been considerable research in order to help define flexible working and family-friendly policies.**

Introduction

In its most recent publication, *Work–Life Balance: Changing patterns in a changing world* (DfEE, 2000), the Government states that 'individuals will flourish if they can strike a proper balance between work and the rest of their lives'. Work–life balance is about developing working practices that benefit both businesses and their employees. It goes on to say that 'business profitability depends on business recruiting and retaining skilled, experienced, productive and motivated people'.

Family-friendly policies have been seen as one of the key measures to help those with family responsibilities. In most cases, these have been directed at helping women with young children to stay in the workplace and to balance their family responsibilities with their working lives. The Government acknowledges the importance of this but says that it is using the term 'work–life balance' to encourage good practice that benefits everyone.

This study was commissioned by the Mid and North Anglia Branch of the Chartered Institute of Personnel and Development (CIPD). The aim was to review the practical arrangements of implementing family-friendly and work–life balance policies of companies in the area, which

includes the cities of Norwich, Peterborough, Cambridge, Great Yarmouth and Bury St Edmunds. Nationally, the CIPD has for some time been concerned to encourage family-friendly working practices. CIPD research into the psychological contract (Guest and Conway, 1998) shows that employees who believe that they have the right balance between life and work are more likely to show significantly more positive attitudes and greater job satisfaction. The study concentrated on family-friendly practices and also looked at wider work–life balance practices where the case study organisations had these arrangements.

Brief review of current research

The Government's promotion of work–life balance policies reflects increasing interest in flexible working practices in the UK and in other countries (Dex and McCulloch, 1995). Some employers have introduced flexibility to meet increasing competition (Casey *et al*, 1997). Others have introduced flexible working in response to employees' needs to reconcile the demands of work and family. Originally these arrangements were mainly aimed at helping the newer workforce of women with children, but gradually the needs of male employees and a wider range of responsibilities have been considered. More recently, the Government has introduced the Fairness at Work proposals to comply with EU

> **'Work–life balance is about developing working practices that benefit both businesses and their employees.'**

Working Time, Part-Time and Parental Leave Directives. Societies increasingly face the challenge of balancing paid work and caring needs (Daly, 1996).

Initiatives like the Opportunity Now campaign have given a boost to generating policies. In its 1998 Annual Report, the Equal Opportunities Commission highlighted the need to promote a better work–life balance for everyone as one of its key priorities. This includes working arrangements that help work–life balancing.

Definitions of family-friendly working

There is a wide range of policies included under the heading of 'family friendly', which makes precise definition difficult. There are policies concerned with employees' hours of work (job sharing, part-time and term-time work, flexitime). Other flexible working practices, including working at or from home, teleworking and self-employment under a contract for specific work, may also benefit work–life balance and be family friendly.

There are policies concerned with leave entitlements (parental and domestic leave, career breaks, and sabbatical leave); and there are various forms of assistance (workplace nurseries, holiday playschemes, childcare financial support or information, enhanced maternity pay) and assistance with particular family responsibilities, eg elderly and dependant care.

There have been attempts to conceptualise family-friendly working arrangements, and the terminology used is now the subject of debate (Lewis and Lewis, 1996). A full discussion of all of the issues is included in Dex and Scheibl (1998).

There are a variety of circumstances leading to the introduction of family-friendly working arrangements. Some were introduced because of formal policies and others have grown up informally. Some provision is designed to benefit a particular group, such as parents with young children, and some benefits a wider range of employees with different needs, including the fulfilment of care for elderly relatives (Forth *et al*, 1997, pp4–5).

Flexible working arrangements such as temporary work and overtime have been used principally to meet the employer's needs for flexibility rather than to meet employees' work–life needs, and can be of most benefit to the employer (Purcell, 1997; Forth *et al*, 1997; Casey *et al*, 1997). Some forms of flexibility, such as annual hours schemes and shift work, can obstruct family life (Heyes, 1997; Purcell, 1997). These practices were not included in the case studies.

It seems most likely that working arrangements will have the best chance of being family friendly in outcome if they have been developed in dialogue with, or in response to, employee concerns. Bevan *et al* (1999) found in a study of small and medium enterprises that family-friendly practices were initially introduced as a response to women employees going on maternity leave, but they developed into wider family-friendly practices. These aspects will be further investigated in the case study analysis.

The extent of family-friendly working policies and practices

There are different ways of measuring the extent of family-friendly arrangements. They can be measured both through the proportion of

> **'It seems most likely that working arrangements will have the best chance of being family friendly in outcome if they have been developed in dialogue with, or in response to, employee concerns.'**

employees who benefit and through the proportion of employers who offer them. Dex and McCulloch (1995) mapped out the extent of flexible employment amongst British workers; approximately one-fifth of men and over one-half of women were in flexible jobs in 1994. The Workplace Employee Relations Survey (WERS) 1998 found that 32 per cent of all employees had access to flexitime arrangements in 1998, 16 per cent of employees had access to job-sharing schemes, 28 per cent to parental leave, 9 per cent to working at or from home, and 4 per cent to a workplace nursery or childcare subsidy (Cully *et al*, 1999). Take-up of some arrangements is low, however. According to analysis of data from the Quarterly Labour Force Survey, only 1 per cent of employed women and 0.1 per cent of men had a job share in 1998 (Dex *et al*, 2000).

There has been significant growth in part-time working and in self-employment, not only because of the need for family-friendly practices, but principally for business reasons. The use of part-time and self-employed workers brings flexibility and reduces the numbers of core full-time staff employed. The number of men working part time has increased from 232,000 in 1981 to 913,000 in 1998, and the number of women working part-time has increased from 3,153,000 in 1975 to 4,512,000 in 1998. The main difference between men and women part-time workers is that women especially rely on part-time work when they have young children, whereas men tend to work part-time when they are also in full-time education, or when they are older (Dex *et al*, 2000).

Table 1 | Access to flexible and family-friendly working arrangements (by gender and sector)

	SECTOR				ALL EMPLOYEES
	PRIVATE		PUBLIC		
	Male	Female	Male	Female	
	% of employees		% of employees		% of employees
Flexitime	24	36	37	39	32
Parental leave	21	30	35	33	28
Job-sharing scheme	6	15	23	34	16
Working from/at home	10	6	13	9	9
Workplace nursery/childcare subsidy	2	3	6	9	4
None of these	57	42	40	34	46

Base: All employees in workplaces of more than 25 employees. Weighted and based on responses from more than 25,457 employees.

Source: Cully *et al*, 1999

Having a policy does not necessarily result in family-friendly practices. Culture and conditions in organisations can be such that employees do not ask to take up the provisions offered for fear that their career prospects may be affected. Equally, small organisations may not need to enact formal policies but may implement family-friendly working practices. Studies have tended to enquire about policies rather than practices. The focus in the case studies is on practices, and several small to medium enterprises (SMEs) are included.

Work–family relationships

Research has shown that there can be benefits and disadvantages to work–family relationships. On the positive side, work provides income, satisfaction and self-worth – needs that become more pressing if absent because of unemployment. However, pressure because of too much work or long hours can create stress and family conflict, especially when demands for care and additional income grow simultaneously. Research indicates that one-third (30 per cent) of all employees would like to work less than 30 hours a week (TUC, 1995). This unmet preference is strongest among women – 53 per cent of women compared with 14 per cent of men want to work less than 30 hours per week. However, the gap between preferred hours and actual hours of work is greatest among those working long hours. A preference for part-time work is also indicated in Curran et al (1993). Research into the reasons for part-time working in small enterprises shows that most chose to work part-time to fit in with other commitments in their lives, especially domestic ones. Only 5.5 per cent of employees worked part-time because of a lack of alternative jobs.

Research by the (former) IPD (1999) shows that one in 10 workers in the survey claimed to work more hours than the Working Time Regulations threshold of 48 hours per week, and almost three-quarters are men. Women who work long hours are more likely than men to work in professional jobs. When asked what would make them work less, a quarter admitted that the matter was in their own hands, and professionals and the health sector are more likely to argue for employing more staff. Three-quarters of those surveyed say that working long hours has some sort of detrimental effect on their job performance.

Take-up

Researchers have pointed out that women are more likely than men to take up family-friendly provisions (Forth et al, 1997) although in the cases of emergency childcare leave and career breaks, the take-up is similar and low for men and women. On the whole, more women than men have access to many of these provisions. However, fathers have been found to take time off around the time of birth of their children; 91 per cent of fathers were found to take on average eight days' leave at this time (Forth et al, 1997), much of it in the form of annual holiday leave.

The low take-up of many family-friendly policies has not been investigated. In some cases, employees may not be at the stage in their lives in which they need to make use of such provisions. They may have chosen other solutions to meet their needs. Others may be unable to afford to reduce their income by taking up reduced hours or career breaks. Alternatively, employees may feel there is some stigma or career penalty attached to taking up such policies, or that their line manager or organisational culture implicitly or even explicitly discourages take-up. This is likely to be more pronounced during recessions and when there is rumour of downsizing. The interviews with employees in the case study organisations provide some information on these questions.

Problems of implementing family-friendly working arrangements

It appears that there are three main levels at which employers may perceive obstacles to the introduction of family-friendly policies (Scheibl and Dex, 1998). Some employers may perceive that the business case is against it. Second, there may be a strong culture that commits some employers to traditional ways of working. Finally, there may be structural constraints imposed by the size of firm, the labour market conditions or the social policy environment that militate against introducing more flexible options. These issues are discussed in detail in Scheibl and Dex (1998).

The recent Policy Studies Institute study reported that equal numbers of British employers saw advantages and disadvantages in providing family-friendly working arrangements. Employers were most likely to perceive benefits for improved staff morale and loyalty together with improved staff relations. The main disadvantages related to increased administration and the disruption through having to cope with staff absences (Forth *et al*, 1997). Other studies have also identified fears of increased costs, for example because more employees would be needed or more cover, as a deterrent (Bailyn, 1993; Holterman, 1995; New Ways to Work, 1993). Employers that do not have

family-friendly working arrangements have also been found to think that these policies will not give them any significant benefits (Forth *et al*, 1997; Wilkinson *et al*, 1997). There is also the matter of selling the arrangements to line managers even when headquarters or senior management has accepted the case for change (Thatcher, 1996). Some of these problems feature in the case studies.

Definitions of work–life balance policies

The Department for Education and Employment discussion document *Work–Life Balance: Changing patterns in a changing world* defines the options available for balancing work and life. These are various part-time arrangements: part-time work; job share; 'v time' work, under which an employee works reduced hours for an agreed period, with a guaranteed return to full-time working at the end of the period; and term-time working. There are also different arrangements for when work is done. These include flexitime, under which employees have a choice within certain limits about when to start and end the working day; compressed hours, which allow an employee to work a full-time job by extending the hours on working days into four days instead of five; and annualised hours, under which employees have to work a required number of hours per year, enabling employees to vary the hours worked in any week, within certain constraints. Finally, there are different arrangements for taking leave, such as extended leave, which allows employees to accumulate certain amounts of annual leave to take together; and sabbatical leave, under which employees accrue entitlement to leave over several years' service, for specific purposes.

> 'The ageing population and reduction in the numbers of young people entering the labour market in the next 10 years will stimulate employers to find new ways of recruiting and retaining skilled and experienced staff.'

It seems clear that there is considerable overlap in the arrangements described by commentators as family friendly, and those defined in the DfEE discussion document as benefiting work–life balance. The difference is mainly to be found in the reasons for employees taking advantage of flexible arrangements and the scale of take-up.

It is likely that many of the concerns that reduce the provision and take-up of family-friendly policies will also affect work–life balance policies, especially part-time working. Employers may consider that there are few significant benefits in having these policies, and employees may be unable to afford to reduce their income by working part time or may be reluctant to take advantage of flexible working because of concerns about how it may affect their career progression.

Work–life balance policies are likely to gain importance because of demographic trends. The ageing population and reduction in the numbers of young people entering the labour market in the next 10 years will stimulate employers to find new ways of recruiting and retaining skilled and experienced staff. This may encourage the recruitment of more part-time workers, including older people, and other forms of flexibility such as using short-term contracts for covering business peaks. Unlike family-friendly policies, this has a wider appeal because it benefits men and women at other stages of their lives. There has also been research that shows that working long hours has an adverse effect on health and family relationships (Cooper and Worrall, 1998). If employers become more accustomed to various forms of flexible working in response to the changing labour market, the status of employees with non-standard working hours may change and this in turn may encourage full-time workers to consider ways of reducing their hours.

Questions for the case studies

As indicated in the brief summary of current research, there are some key questions to explore in the case studies. Did the case study organisations consider that there were any structural constraints against the provision of family-friendly arrangements? Did the case study organisations find in practice that there were business benefits in having family-friendly arrangements, and if so what were they? Conversely, what disruption problems and costs had been found?

As regards take-up, did employees in the case studies consider that the company culture militated against their applying to work more flexibly? Did they consider that there was an unmet need, and what factors deterred others from taking up family-friendly arrangements? What was the attitude of managers?

Finally, looking ahead, are the case study organisations expecting to increase the extent of family-friendly and work–life balance arrangements, and what lessons can others learn from the experience in the case studies?

2 | Focus of the study

◪ **The case study organisations represent a diverse group of small, medium and large Mid and North Anglian industries, including the growing knowledge-based high technology sectors, manufacturing and food.**

◪ **There are a wide variety of practices included in the case studies, with the greatest emphasis being given by the participants to various flexible working practices such as part-time jobs and self-employment, which were seen as the most significant adjustments being made to meet employees' needs for work–life balance.**

Overview of case study organisations

Although current research raises certain questions to be explored (see *Questions for the case studies* on page 6), the main purpose of this study is to provide practical information by investigating the implementation of family-friendly and work–life balance arrangements, any practical problems that were experienced, and how these were overcome. The studies will also provide insights into the critical conditions for the successful implementation of family-friendly and work–life balance arrangements.

We aimed to have a cross-section of 12 case studies in different industrial sectors and sizes, covering a variety of occupations and functions in Mid and North Anglia. It was thought to be particularly important to include small and medium employers, because it was expected that they might provide useful lessons. It is claimed that small firms lack the flexibility required for varying working hours, working time and leave arrangements. This seemed to be confirmed by the WERS data (Cully *et al*, 1999), which indicates that family-friendly policies are more prevalent in large organisations, especially in the public sector.

We also wanted to examine how our case study organisations benefited from the introduction of family-friendly or work–life balance arrangements, and whether they had experienced any of the difficulties such as disruption and administrative costs found in the Policy Studies Institute research (Forth *et al*, 1997), and if so how these were overcome. Where possible, we explored the attitudes and experiences of employees and managers.

The case study sample

One problem inherent in the case study methodology is the extent to which participants are typical. In this study, those who agreed to take part described mostly positive experiences. Those with problematic or unsatisfactory experiences are less likely to agree to participate. Several declined to take part in the study because they felt that they had no good examples of family-friendly arrangements. For example, one small firm that formerly had employees working from home abandoned the arrangement because it failed, mainly because the employees felt too isolated. Another said that their male employees were interested only in doing as much overtime as they

'Although these case studies do not represent the full range of industries that are the most likely to have family-friendly practices, they illustrate many of the issues raised in the summary of current research.'

could. The study has concentrated on arrangements that are working well, from which some useful lessons have emerged.

In addition, some industries that are the biggest employers of part-time women workers, such as retail and distribution, and others such as financial services, are not included, although there are two examples from the NHS, another large employer of part-time women staff. Also included are several knowledge-based industries, which are among the emerging and strong sectors in the region's economy, including bio-technology, and information and communications technology.

However, the occupations represented do include some of those with the highest levels of part-time working for both men and women: sales, other occupations and personal and protective services.

Although these case studies do not represent the full range of industries that are the most likely to have family-friendly practices, they illustrate many of the issues raised in the summary of current research.

Practices included

The types of family-friendly and work–life balance arrangements in the 12 case study organisations are outlined in Table 2.

The practices in Table 2 cover most of the arrangements described and analysed in current research.

Table 2 | Number of organisations with each practice

Type of practice	No. of organisations
Part-time work	12
Job share	9
Self-employed	5
Term-time work	3
Compressed hours	1
Seasonal work	7
Flexitime with and without time off in lieu	11 (2 formal schemes)
Working from/at home	12 (2 formal schemes)
Career breaks	3
Sabbaticals	4
Extended leave	11
Parental and paternity leave	12
Extended maternity leave	7
Time off for domestic emergencies	12
Unpaid leave	11
Holiday playschemes	1
Childcare allowances	2
Childcare advice and information	3
Advice on other domestic provision	Informal
Counselling	6
Support networks	2

> **'Most of the case study organisations saw part-time working as the most significant family-friendly arrangement.'**

Extent of arrangements

The extent of the arrangements varied considerably. All of the case study organisations offered various additional paid and unpaid leave arrangements, for domestic and other emergencies. In many cases the practice or arrangement was described as 'informal' and 'on request', especially in the case of flexitime, working from home and granting unpaid leave. Informal working from home arrangements were normally for professional and managerial staff, who needed to work uninterrupted on discrete tasks such as drafting reports. There were two examples of formal working from home arrangements, under which the company recognised the place of work as the employee's home. The extended leave arrangements were limited to four or five days. Two had formal flexitime policies.

Most of the case study organisations saw part-time working as the most significant family-friendly arrangement. All had employees who worked part-time to meet domestic requirements, and these workers were almost all women with young and school-aged children. Two organisations also used self-employed freelance workers, and one employed marketing staff who worked from home. The latter were examples of practices that help balance work and life and were used by men.

The two NHS organisations and one food manufacturer relied heavily on part-time workers to meet operational needs or production peaks. The other case study organisations made limited provision for part-time work and did not rely heavily on it.

Table 3 | Categorisation by part-time and flexible work of case study organisations

Size	Type of user		
	High	Medium	Low
Medium			Leo Electron Microscopy
Large			Aventis Crop Science
Large		British Sugar	
Medium			Bidwells
Large	Norfolk & Norwich NHS Trust		
Large	Norfolk Mental Health Care NHS Trust		
Large			Rebus
Large	Gilchris		
Large			Johnson Matthey
Large			Ridgeons
Small		Leathes Prior	
Small			Public Administration

3 | Reasons for implementing family-friendly practices

◨ **Reasons given for introducing family-friendly practices included: the need to retain skilled staff, particularly women with young children; the need to meet operational requirements; and the desire to be seen as a good employer.**

◨ **Recent legislation had caused the participants to review their leave entitlements, but leave was not seen as significant for retaining employees as the introduction of flexible working such as part-time employment.**

◨ **In many cases, practices such as part-time and other flexible working were introduced informally in response to employee requests rather than as a result of a formal policy.**

Table 4 | Principal reasons for family-friendly arrangements (frequency: more than one reason given)

Reason	Number
Retain skilled/experienced staff	9
Company ethics	3
Recruitment problems	3
To be a good employer	2
To meet operational needs	2
To meet staff needs	2
Head office initiative	2
Help staff travel difficulties	1

The majority of reasons given in Table 4 are business related, and in fact all respondents gave at least one business reason for introducing a specific practice.

Retaining skills and experience

The main reason for the adoption of family-friendly arrangements, given by nine organisations as the most important, was the need to retain the skills and experience of valued employees. This was also the reason for employing men on part-time or self-employed contracts. One respondent said:

We need to retain qualified professional staff.

Another said:

We noticed that we were losing too many good women.

Women are increasingly becoming a breadwinner. We have to recognise this. But they have more difficulty with their careers if they have children.

> **'The main reason for the adoption of family-friendly arrangements ... was the need to retain the skills and experience of valued employees.'**

Similarly:

It was a reaction to people not returning from maternity leave.

Family-friendly arrangements were also important for meeting difficulties in recruiting women. An NHS HR manager said:

There is always a problem recruiting nurses. The holiday playscheme is an aid to recruitment.

Good practice

Other reasons given by respondents were the need to be seen as a good employer and maintain good employee relations. A typical comment was:

We want to maintain good employee relations.

Another comment was:

Our HR strategy is based on the psychological contract. We are trying to be more progressive and show that we value employees.

For other companies, being family-friendly conformed to the company culture or ethos:

We have an open company culture. People don't feel threatened by raising their family problems.

And:

We recognise that when we employ someone, they are part of a family. This is at the centre of company culture.

The three public sector organisations, all of which had long-standing family-friendly policies and practices, introduced them to comply with a central policy or a senior-level initiative.

Operational requirements

In three organisations, it was necessary to have part-time working to meet production or operational requirements, and this also made it possible to meet the needs of people with young families. One food manufacturer had found it increasingly difficult to recruit additional temporary staff to cover busy seasonal production periods; after informal consultations with staff and an assessment of the production implications by the planning department, it introduced term-time working. In the two NHS trusts, part-time working and self-employment have long been essential to recruit and retain highly trained staff and to cover twilight and night shifts.

Impact of legislation

None of the respondents gave recent legislation as the main reason for introducing family-friendly arrangements. This was because they considered part-time, flexitime or reduced hours working to be the most significant family-friendly practices, and not parental leave or leave for domestic emergencies. All the case study organisations had reviewed their parental leave and domestic leave provisions to ensure that they complied with the minimum standards laid down in the Employment Relations Act 1999, and several offered paid paternity leave or improved their provisions because of the legislation. One respondent used

> **'It is notable that the majority of the case study organisations were reactive and introduced family-friendly arrangements ... in response to requests by employees or because of losses of key staff.'**

legislation as one reason for introducing wider changes to establish the company as a family-friendly employer. The main reasons for issuing guidelines on new practices were a commitment to good practice and a response to employee concerns raised in an employee opinion survey.

Influence of trade unions

Five of the case study organisations were unionised, but unions were not seen as a significant influence on the development of family-friendly practices. In one NHS trust, family-friendly policies were discussed at the local Whitley Council before implementation, and their involvement was described as 'a factor, but difficult to quantify'.

In the other NHS trust, unions were very keen on childcare facilities and were 'pushing' for it.

A private sector organisation said that unions were informed before a new family-friendly policy was introduced and were 'very positive.'

Reactive or proactive

It is notable that the majority of the case study organisations were reactive and introduced family-friendly arrangements, such as part-time work, in response to requests by employees or because of losses of key staff.

In the words of one HR manager, 'It was a response to female-driven work requirements.'

Several of the reactive organisations had no formal policies nor criteria, apart from those required by the legislation. They considered requests for variations in time and hours worked on a case-by-case basis, an approach that puts the onus on employees to make out a case or on HR staff to negotiate with departmental managers. Different assumptions were made about the suitability of different functions to be organised into part-time jobs. The departmental or line manger has the final decision, and there is a risk that many will be reluctant to introduce different working practices. There is also a risk of different considerations being used, giving rise to inconsistencies or unfairness. (See *Influencing managers* on page 19 and *Experience of managers* on page 25.)

Three organisations were proactive in introducing family-friendly practices. One of these saw family-friendly practices and the idea of work–life balance as part of a wider change, moving to a culture of employee involvement and empowerment. This organisation had carried out informal research into the needs of women returning from maternity leave, to inform their policy development, and responses in an employee opinion survey indicated that employees had concerns about work/home balance.

4 | Experiences, benefits and disadvantages

☒ **The case study organisations reported significant business benefits from implementing family-friendly policies.**

☒ **The case study organisations reported that employees who worked part-time and other non-standard arrangements had higher productivity than other employees, and some did a full-time job in three or four days.**

☒ **People whose work–life balance needs had been met were found to be highly motivated and committed to the company.**

☒ **Specific provisions such as a holiday playscheme and a childcare subsidy were a bonus in recruitment and retention.**

☒ **Although there were additional costs from employing part-timers, such as extra co-ordination and training, these were felt to be outweighed by the gains.**

The business benefits

All the case study participants said that they had found significant business benefits in implementing family-friendly and work–life balance arrangements (see Table 5). It is interesting to note that many of the benefits experienced were not anticipated in the reasons given for introducing family-friendly arrangements.

Most respondents said that part-time employees, and self-employed workers in particular, had far higher productivity than other workers. Some typical comments were:

She does as much in three days as a full-time person.

We get better productivity from part-timers because they are more motivated.

Managers are very pleased with part-timers because they are very dedicated.

Table 5 | Benefits from family-friendly practices (frequency: more than one reason given)

Benefits	Number
Increased productivity	4
Higher commitment/better motivation/more reliable	5
More flexibility	6
Improved retention	5
Reduced recruitment	5
Lower absenteeism	2
Improved customer service	4
Reduced costs (fewer temporary staff)	4
Improved employee relations	4

> **'All the case study participants said that they had found significant business benefits in implementing family-friendly and work–life balance arrangements.'**

There were also important gains experienced in improved operational flexibility. This applied to part-time workers and to the self-employed. One respondent said of their use of self-employed professionals:

We can expand or contract when we need to. It allows us to get a team together quickly.

Part-timers were often willing to work additional hours to help provide cover, as the following comments indicate:

Part-timers can be brought in as an additional cover. We can phone them at home and they will come in at short notice and do additional days.

We get better cover from two part-timers.

It works well. We get cover and they also work full time to cover holidays.

These comments were strongly confirmed by the experiences of managers, especially in service functions. For example, an office services manager with two part-time women staff trained them to be multi-skilled, deployed them to cover for holidays, sickness and unforeseen events, and felt he could offer a higher level of service for longer hours. He attended a seminar on family-friendly practices, which, he said, had opened his eyes to the possibilities of varying from the norm, although before then he had been against having part-time staff. A manager with seven part-time staff described the operational flexibility given by having staff who would vary their working days to cover for holidays and sickness. He was also able to extend the hours for which his departmental services were available. An NHS team manager said that using part-time staff gave added

flexibility and benefited the whole team. If part-time staff were multi-skilled, they could take up cases to cover for leave or sickness. It meant that staff had lower case loads and this helped reduce pressure.

Typical comments from managers were:

It gives flexibility to us both. It meets her needs for fewer hours, and we maintain continuity and retain her knowledge.
(Manager of self-employed professional woman)

She does as much as she did when she worked full time. We retain her skills and knowledge and save on training and recruitment costs.
(Sales and marketing manager of part-time marketing assistant)

People work better if they work hours which suit their situation. They are less likely to move on if we can accommodate their wishes.
(Training and administration manager of several part-time staff)

The last comment picks up on another advantage of family-friendly practices. The case study organisations found that providing flexibility of working hours or days to people resulted in improved motivation and commitment. Some comments on part-time employees were:

Very dedicated and loyal.

They are not clock-watchers.

They are more reliable than full-time staff. (term-time employees)

They have to sell themselves and their expertise. (self-employed workers)

> **'The case study organisations found that providing flexibility of working hours or days to people resulted in improved motivation and commitment.'**

Several organisations said that they believed that absenteeism was lower for part-timers and as a result of flexitime, but only two had measured this. Similarly, several said that their use of temporary staff had reduced as a result of employing part-time workers, but again most had not separately measured this.

Family-friendly arrangements were advertised as significant attractions in an NHS Job Fair. The promotional flyer lists 'Flexibility in work options', 'Holiday playschemes at nearby school' and 'Nursery planned at new hospital' as three out of the six reasons for working for the trust.

Improvements to customer services were reported by four organisations. The accumulated hours worked by two or more part-time staff allowed these companies to be open to customers earlier and later than was possible with the equivalent full-time staff working overtime. One said that flexitime helped provide better customer service in outfacing areas early and late, which was when it was wanted. In two professional firms, part-time staff were flexible in order to maintain client links and were available by telephone and e-mail at home. It was felt that these staff were as accessible as full-time staff because their time was devoted solely to clients.

Disruption costs and disadvantages

Table 6 gives the most frequently cited problems and costs. Five case study organisations considered that the problems involved in specified types of non-standard working outweighed the benefits. One had found that job share did not work effectively because of the difficulties in maintaining client continuity. They had moved to self-employment for professional staff who

wanted a shorter week, and this had proved more effective because the individual was contracted to work on specified projects with specific clients. Another found it difficult to recruit the other half of a job share. A third found poor take-up of the career break scheme because it did not meet employees' needs for re-entering the workplace after maternity. There was insufficient contact during the career break and people found it difficult to keep up with technical changes. It was more effective for them to work part-time for two days per week. Two organisations tried working from home, but found it difficult to manage because the employees felt too isolated.

Table 6 | Reported disruption costs and disadvantages (frequency: more than one reason given)

Costs/disadvantage	Number
Co-ordination/cover	9
Difficulties in persuading managers	10
Additional training or administration of training	7
Maintaining client/customer continuity	2
Costs of provision of benefit/facility/equipment	6
Keeping in touch (career breaks)	1
Low take-up	1
Recruitment of job sharers (difficult)	1
Isolation (working from home)	2

Although there were disadvantages, in practice, apart from the five specific examples given above, the case study organisations did not see these as significant deterrents to continuing to implement family-friendly arrangements. Their experience suggests that the arrangements worked well if they met employees' and the business needs.

For example, there was a need for additional co-ordination of the work of two part-time staff, the costs of an overlap of their days in, and for additional training or for training to be arranged on days suitable for part-time staff. However:

The extra costs were not enough to be significant.

The added value outweighs the extra administration and costs involved.

We see training as an investment.

The extra costs are lost in the overheads.

The extra costs of training and co-ordination are offset by savings in the recruitment process.

A company that had term-time working allocated resources to finding out about each local school's extra holidays and closures so that they could foresee absences and plan production schedules accordingly.

The need for co-ordination of shared work of part-timers was acknowledged to be important, but in several cases this was the responsibility of the staff who shared responsibilities and work:

Individuals must sort out their own cover arrangements.

They manage their own cover.

Self-management of co-ordination tended to be done by staff in teams, either in support and service functions, or in research and development. Where the part-time staff were in professional and managerial functions, co-ordination was done by support staff, such as secretaries. It was agreed by all those interviewed that communications and co-ordination between full-time colleagues and part-time staff, people working flexitime and people working shorter hours, made the difference between success and failure. It was necessary for the part-timer to plan on a daily basis what tasks were outstanding and to ensure that a colleague was prepared to deal with any matters that came up in their absence, or to have a system for referring all such matters to the part-timer at home. (For further details of practical arrangements see *Experience of managers* on page 25.)

In several cases, part-time staff had been trained in several functions so that the company could use their skills flexibly in different sections to cover for absenteeism and holidays or to provide additional resources to cope with peaks in work flows. This also tended to be where they worked in teams.

Two organisations had paid the cost of installing a telephone line to enable the employee to work from home. This had improved their accessibility to customers/clients and was seen as a good investment.

The most significant and identifiable cost incurred was for the holiday playscheme organised by an NHS trust. This was almost self-financing, apart from an annual subsidy of £4,500. It had been set up over 20 years ago and was so well established that it had not been necessary to justify the costs. It was seen as essential for the recruitment and retention of trained professional nurses.

> **'All the case study organisations … found that managers were reluctant to accept variations in the standard working hours because they assumed that it would lead to problems.'**

Influencing managers

All the case study organisations had problems in persuading managers to accept non-standard working arrangements. They found that managers were reluctant to accept variations in the standard working hours because they assumed that it would lead to problems. An HR manager said that assumptions made by managers in her company before the arrangements were put in place were:

Customers will complain, there will be lack of flexibility and lower productivity, and the business will suffer.

In fact, she said that the reverse occurred.

Other HR managers had encountered managers with strong negative opinions of family-friendly arrangements, or found that older managers with a more 'controlling' style were against more flexible working.

Managers don't like it because they say it will cause disruption to the shop floor.

(Personnel manager of term-time working)

In fact, the shifts had adjusted to the change and it was working smoothly.

Some managers question whether it is practical. But they have to consider the consequences of saying no. The person would be seriously disaffected.

(Training manager)

In organisations with published family-friendly policies, HR managers had done presentations or briefings to promote the new working arrangements. Many, however, were introducing new arrangements in response to requests by

employees. In order to convince managers, it was important to think through the consequences of the change, show how it would work and make out a case for it. Managers needed to be aware of the options. It was important to think how to get a positive response and avoid a 'no' because it had not been thought through. One respondent stressed the importance of professional HR involvement in dealing with requests for variations in working arrangements.

It became easier when there were some successful examples:

If it works well, others see the positive results and it sells itself.

(HR manager)

The attitude of managers has changed now because it has worked.

(HR manager)

It has been a very positive experience, which managers can see.

(Personnel manager)

The interviews with HR managers suggests that they have faced significant opposition from managers and have used a range of negotiating tactics to influence and persuade them to accept changes in working arrangements. It is also noticeable that, for many, the negotiations were in response to requests by valued employees. These people have, in a sense, become pioneers because their success is used as an argument to smooth the way for subsequent change.

Small and medium firms' experiences

As indicated in *The extent of family-friendly working policies and practices* on page 2, quantitative research indicates that family-friendly policies are most prevalent in the public sector and in larger companies. One aim of the case studies was to investigate the practices of small and medium-sized enterprises (SMEs). Four of the case study organisations are small and medium firms. Two have fewer than 100 employees, two have fewer than 400 employees, and all have a high proportion of qualified professional or technical employees.

All four introduced flexible practices principally in order to retain qualified staff, particularly women. One public sector organisation had formal policies and criteria for family-friendly working and the remaining three had introduced family-friendly practices in response to requests by staff. Two firms have male staff working flexibly as self-employed consultants.

The nature of the work done by the four SMEs was significant. Three were providing professional services. They considered that they gained from having flexible working arrangements because clients wanted their services outside standard business hours. Thus by having professional and support staff who worked part time and flexitime, they were able to provide additional cover. Staff could vary their hours and see clients after 6.00pm, or be available by telephone at home. The success of this depended on staff being: adaptable; prepared to be on call; willing to vary their part-time hours; or willing to work after core hours as required. A fourth SME employed highly qualified technical and scientific specialists. The firm said that it would find it difficult to find replacement staff with the necessary training, knowledge and experience. They saw flexible working practices as part of an open company culture, which helped develop loyalty, and in which staff had respect for each other. In research and

development, flexibility of hours and times was sorted out in teams through negotiations with colleagues, and in other areas it was considered according to the requirements of the job.

The four SMEs undoubtedly saw business benefits in having family-friendly practices. One said:

It is very competitive in this sector. We would not do it if it were uneconomic.

In two professional firms the costs of flexible working arrangements were considered along with other considerations each time a specific request for a variation in hours was made.

All four firms considered that one of the criteria for the success of different working practices was in having detailed built-in arrangements for cover and adaptable, flexible attitudes on the part of individuals and their colleagues. The attitudes of individuals were crucial in making the arrangements work well for the business.

The experience of small and medium-sized firms in the case studies is similar to the findings in Bevan *et al* (1999); they reported considerable benefits, including improved productivity and commitment, and the employees reported increased loyalty and better work–life balance.

Employees' experiences

In all except one case study, interviews were held with employees who worked non-standard hours or benefited in other ways from arrangements that helped work–life balance. The majority of interviewees worked part time or reduced hours. There were also interviews with self-employed staff, staff working from home and staff who utilised childcare provision. In total 33 people were

'The pattern in the case studies tends to confirm that flexibility and family-friendly practices are more likely to be taken up by women with childcare needs.'

interviewed – 29 women and four men. Twenty-five of the 29 women who worked part time, reduced hours or were self-employed, did so because they had young children. Four women worked part-time and the four men worked at home or were self-employed because they wanted a better work–life balance. The pattern in the case studies tends to confirm that flexibility and family-friendly practices are more likely to be taken up by women with childcare needs.

Employees were asked about the benefits of family-friendly practices to them and their employers, the problems, and the lessons from the success. Perceptions of colleagues' and managers' attitudes were also explored.

Benefits to employees

The benefits described by interviewees largely depended on the reasons for their different working arrangements or use of a particular provision.

Women with young children tended to work part time – two, three or four days per week – or reduced hours, such as two full days and two or three six-hour days. They all felt that such arrangements enabled them to balance childcare with staying in the labour market and keeping up with developments.

I see more of my child and he sees me when I'm not always rushing. I can keep in touch with the working environment and with technological changes.

(Marketing assistant, 20 hours per week)

It fits in with my children's school times. I can take them four days per week, and my husband takes them on the fifth day. I have spent 16 years

building up my career, and I can keep my hand in and be up to date.

(Senior designer, 25 hours per week)

I can spend time with my son and keep my career going.

(Personnel manager, three days per week)

I get one day with my child at home. I have a better work–life balance and am under less pressure.

(Professional, four days per week)

There were so many demands on my time, and I could not admit it was too much. Now I have more control over my time and can use it more effectively. I can be with my children in the day and work evenings.

(Self-employed professional)

I work more enthusiastically because I'm not stressed out.

(Accounts assistant, three days per week)

I'm more productive in my four days here because I am more relaxed.

(Professional, four days per week)

Reduced pressure and freedom to do other things in life were benefits described by people at different stages in their lives who worked reduced hours:

I could not detach myself from the political side of corporate life. Now I concentrate on my profession and have a better work–life balance.

(Man, self-employed professional)

There is less stress.

(Woman, self-employed professional)

> '**Employees whose working arrangements had been changed to meet family and life circumstances clearly felt that they were being granted a favour and were under an obligation to perform well … .**'

I have time for my own activities. I am renovating a house and garden.

(Woman, part-time secretary)

It's not just for young 'mums'. I don't work such long hours now because I want to put something back into the community.

(Man, full-time manager)

I have the freedom to refresh myself and I can go out when I've finished my work. I am under less pressure and am freed from corporate politics and hassle.

(Man, marketing manager, works from home)

I want to do other things with my life. Why should we work forever?

(Woman manager, four days per week)

Business benefits

The benefits described by employees mirrored many of those seen by their employers.

Loyalty and motivation

Employees whose working arrangements had been changed to meet family and life circumstances clearly felt that they were being granted a favour and were under an obligation to perform well and be beyond criticism. This applied equally to working mothers, older women and to the men in the sample. It appears that they felt visible and therefore vulnerable to comment and fault finding. Interviewees were keen to stress that their work quality and productivity were high. They also stressed that they took all possible steps to avoid disruption in their absence. These feelings were expressed as follows by a man working as a self-employed part-time consultant:

It is a privilege to work part time, not a right. It is a moral contract and I am determined to deliver value to the company.

Other comments included:

I put in one thousand per cent diligence. It was my choice to become part time and the company is being accommodating. I appreciate being treated as an individual and it is a good message to give to others.

(Woman, part-time receptionist)

I have to be flexible. I am prepared to work longer hours to get the work out. You can't tell a client that you'll do it when you can.

(Woman, part-time financial services assistant)

I'm trying to prove that I can do it. Women with children have to be better organised and more focused than other staff. The company stood by me and I am willing to put in extra to ensure that the job is done.

(Woman, part-time key accounts executive)

I was the first part-timer at my level. The pressure is on me to get the work done. It's critical to get as much done as I can. I don't waste any time, I am very focused, every minute is important.

(Woman, part-time personnel manager)

Productivity, flexibility and quality

Many interviewees were doing the same job and producing the same amount of work as they were before reducing their working hours or days, but were being paid less because of their reduced hours. This was not uppermost in their minds when asked about their experience. They were more likely to see the economic gain for the company as evidence that the arrangement worked well. They were also anxious to show that their flexibility was not at the company's expense. Part-time staff in particular felt under pressure to perform well, offer flexibility and be above criticism:

Clients get an improved quality of service and a more experienced professional for less.

(Woman, self-employed professional)

I do as much in the time as when I was full time, for less money. My manager would like to pay me more because he thinks I am used as cheap labour.

(Woman, part-time marketing assistant)

I can do the work in four days.

(Woman, part-time marketing assistant)

It's cheaper for the company. I do a full-time job in fewer hours. They are gaining full-time work for less.

(Woman, part-time payroll assistant)

The company gets total cover from us. We sort out our times and cover for each other. It's better than having full-time people: we can be more flexible and we have capacity.

(Woman, part-time administration services)

I work at it more than the company. There is a cost to you. When I work in a team, I am very conscious that I am the only one with a young dependant. I want to contribute and therefore there is pressure on me to get the work done. I don't waste any time...it's critical to get as much work done as I can. The company gets more out of me, I'm giving good value.'

(Woman, part-time personnel manager)

I'm trying to prove that I can do it. Women with children have to be better organised and more focused than other people.

(Woman, part-time sales and marketing executive)

I do see clients on my day off. I'm using my own time.

(Woman, part-time professional)

Disadvantages for employees

Most part-time women did not see their reduced earnings as the main disadvantage. Only one referred to financial difficulties, saying:

I really struggled financially. Balancing work and life is very demanding and the burden falls on women.

Employees who worked part-time or reduced hours were more likely to answer by reference to their work. For example, several were aware that maintaining continuity with customers and clients when they were not at work could be a potential problem and could lead to client dissatisfaction. They had all put in place arrangements for briefing colleagues or for being contacted at home:

When I go I tell the administrative assistant about things which might come up and she rings me if necessary.

(Woman, senior designer, 25 hours per week)

Continuity and communications could be a problem. It's important to record all messages and not to clash with the other half.

(Woman, job-share receptionist)

> **'Most part-time employees … felt that they were not taken as seriously as their full-time colleagues, or were not seen as part of the team.'**

Loss of continuity can be a problem. I changed my days of work to give better continuity, and I take work home.

(Woman, part-time personnel manager)

Continuity was a problem when I worked two and a half days per week. Now I work half days every day and this is better, because I am in for core hours.

(Woman, part-time credit control)

Another frequently mentioned problem was workload, especially for women who had formerly been full time. They worked more intensively and in a more focused way and often did a full-time workload:

I work through my lunches to cope. I don't want to leave before it is all finished.

(Woman, part-time sales administrator)

The company gets more out of me than other employees.

(Woman, part-time accounts assistant)

I stay late and work through lunch hours if needed.

(Woman, part-time sales and marketing executive)

Career progression

Some more senior part-time women felt that they experienced disadvantages in their career development and progression. For example, it was difficult to attend team-building sessions that were arranged on their days out, or they could not attend team events that started early or went on late. Several mothers of young children felt that they were unable to progress, but accepted that this may be the price they had to pay until their dependants were older. One woman said:

The problem for me is progression. I applied for promotion and was told I was suitable but only if I worked a full week. I thought the job could be done in four days. I was torn; I would regret whatever decision I made. I was angry at being put in a position to choose.

Other comments were:

Some think I couldn't go further in a more senior role. Society has a long way to go on this. Part-time work is not acceptable. It is badly paid and has low status.

Negative attitudes

Most part-time employees, including those who had previously worked for the company for many years full time, felt that they were not taken as seriously as their full-time colleagues, or were not seen as part of the team. There were references to comments and resentment from colleagues.

I'm seen as different, not quite part of the group; an outsider, more like a 'temp'.

(Woman, part time, with 16 years' full-time experience)

I'm not taken as seriously. I'm seen as a mother and judgements are made on this and not on me as someone who wants to move on. Some of the men think that I've made my choice and should stay home.

(Woman, part-time accounts executive, 14 years' experience)

I feel undervalued. I would like to be valued: what I do is important, not the hours I work.

(Woman, part-time IT projects manager)

> **'Managers felt that responding to employees' family or work–life balance needs had a pay-off as staff were more motivated, more adaptable and displayed a better attitude to their work.'**

Part-time staff are not valued. It's seen as a 'little job' or 'working for pin money'. The stigma is still there.

(Woman, part-time receptionist, ten years' experience)

The attitudes of colleagues could also be negative. For example:

There is some resentment, a colleague commented for example, 'I wish I had an excuse to leave on time.'

(Woman, part time)

One male manager who worked from home said that people find it difficult to adapt to the arrangement, and put it succinctly:

The biggest problem is guilt. People ring me when I'm not supposed to be at work, early in the morning, and make comments such as 'are you dressed yet?', or later in the day: 'you can't work in the garden'.

Experience of managers

All the managers interviewed were very positive about their experience of part-time or other forms of flexible working. In general their comments echoed those of their staff. They found the use of part-time staff gave flexibility, extended and additional cover. It enabled them to provide their services for longer hours and to meet holiday and sickness absence. A manager of professional staff said that using part-time and self-employed people increased creativity because there was more diversity of experience and different perspectives.

Managers felt that responding to employees' family or work–life balance needs had a pay-off as staff were more motivated, more adaptable and displayed a better attitude to their work. One

manager with several part-time staff, including a man who had left a career as a retail branch manager to have a less pressurised life, said:

People work better if they can work hours which suit their situation. They are less likely to move on if we can accommodate their wishes.

This was echoed by another manager who said:

It doesn't matter when they do the hours. If we can be flexible, they give more in return. They look on the company more favourably and are more loyal and committed.

Part-time and job-share arrangements also reduced the need for using temporary staff, which saved money and reduced disruption from having to train new people.

Once having experienced the benefits of flexibility, managers could see possibilities for extending flexible arrangements, and in some cases became advocates for changes in practice. They could see that there were various stages in life when people needed flexibility. For example, flexible working benefits older staff, who had problems of caring for elderly parents. They thought that there was scope for much greater flexibility in all departments, but said that managers in other departments tended to assume that 'my area is different' and they prefer full-time fixed hours. A typical comment was:

Part-time working is not liked because managers believe it is difficult to cover when the member of staff is absent.

All these managers felt that their company was not doing enough to publicise the benefits of part-time and other variations on working arrangements. One commented that other managers were not aware of the possibilities and no one outside his department saw how it worked. Another said that part-time working was appreciated only when a department had experienced the benefits. One said that it was important for there to be a favourable attitude by senior managers.

Practical lessons

There were some practical lessons that had been learned in the management of flexible working. Again, managers' experience mirrored that of their staff. Good communications and co-ordination were essential where several people shared a function. It was important to work it through and think about informal as well as formal communications. One professional firm with self-employed staff used a video link to keep in touch with them and for them to link with other offices when they worked at home. These staff were explicitly made part of a team so that the whole team had to sort out the working arrangements together and they were responsible for making sure they worked well. This was the approach of other managers with part-time staff in their departments. It was necessary to plan ahead to ensure that meetings and company and staff communications were done during core hours or were repeated for people not at work on the day. There was a little more co-ordination needed than for a department in which everyone worked the same hours.

Although all accepted that it was a little more expensive to have several part-time staff (one estimate was 25 per cent more), this was offset by reduced recruitment and related training costs, by reduced use of temporary staff, by increased

productivity, and by the retention of knowledge and skills. They believed that recruitment difficulties would increase and part-time and other flexible working arrangements would grow when managers were faced with problems of getting skilled full-time staff.

Unmet needs and future trends

Human resource managers and employees were asked whether they thought that there was an unmet demand for part-time and other forms of flexible working. None of the respondents had carried out any recent analysis of potential demand. But when asked about demand, all agreed that they expected there to be an increase in take-up, particularly of part-time work and flexitime, as knowledge of the current successful arrangements spread. They considered that there were many in the present workforce who would like to work shorter hours, but the nature of their jobs prevented them from doing so. Several HR managers thought that flexitime schemes and part-time work were easier to manage in non-production areas, in functions where work is organised among teams or allocated by task, because there was more control over individual work flows. They said that production managers had more traditional ideas about the need for managerial control. Managers and HR managers interviewed in this study all reported hearing other managers' comments, such as:

It wouldn't work in production.

It would be more difficult for managers.

It can't work in customer services because it has to be open all hours.

'Several employees interviewed felt that their employer could do more to establish the scope for more flexible working and to assess employees' needs.'

But part-time working and flexitime systems were operated successfully in all these functions in other case study companies. This suggests that some of the case study organisations were not open minded about the possibilities of extending family-friendly arrangements to existing staff.

Some human resource managers considered that part-time work would increase primarily because of demographic factors and the increase in women's participation in work. All respondents employed increasing numbers of young women managers and expected that before long these women would have families and the company would soon have to face the choice of varying their hours or losing their experience. Several expressed interest in the economics of providing a workplace crèche, as there were several key staff on maternity leave. More generally, they were aware of demographic change, the 'ageing' population and the reduction in the numbers of new entrants to the labour market, and were expecting to face recruitment problems, at least in some skilled sectors. One way of meeting shortages was to recruit staff on more flexible working arrangements. With this in mind one case study organisation decided to offer term-time and weekend shifts. They held an open day and there was a great deal of interest. They now have a waiting list of people wanting this work and other local companies visit them to find out how it works.

Changing social attitudes was another factor. Managers' attitudes were changing, especially where there were successful examples of flexible working arrangements. Companies with an employee-centred culture in which the business was built around the skills of highly trained and qualified people were more likely to be looking

ahead and trying to anticipate how attitudes to work are changing. These same companies were making links between family-friendly practices – primarily driven by the needs of women with children – and work–life balance.

Employees were also well aware that there was an unfulfilled desire for more flexible working arrangements. They said that many of their friends and colleagues would like to work shorter hours or have greater flexibility, particularly women with children. Typical comments were:

Many more would work part-time if they could. They are either overstretched or don't work at all. The company recently advertised a part-time job and there were over 600 applicants. There is a big gap in the market which is not being exploited by companies.

Many more would vary their hours if they could. Companies should do more to accommodate working mothers with children.

Several employees interviewed felt that their employer could do more to establish the scope for more flexible working and to assess employees' needs. One part-time worker said that, although her employer offered her a good deal, she felt that there were many departments that could be more flexible without losing out at all, but nothing had been done to find out what could be available. Another woman spoke about the difficulty of asking to work reduced hours and felt that it was much better if the company took the initiative. She said:

Employers should offer flexible working arrangements to current staff as an option. It's very difficult to raise it yourself, because if you do, it signals that you are 'a problem' and have a lack of commitment. As a working mother, there are so many demands on your time, but I could not admit that I was under pressure.

(Woman, professional)

The feeling that more should be done to enable staff to vary their working arrangements was expressed by several other employees. It was most marked in organisations in which arrangements were ad hoc and staff had to negotiate any variation themselves. One part-time woman professional asked for several years before she was able to persuade her director to agree to reduce her hours. She commented:

Companies need to change. There is an ageing workforce and they will have to encourage older workers to stay in the labour market. One way of doing this is by being flexible about the hours worked.

Another woman said:

Companies should listen to their staff and pick up their wider needs, and not assume that their arrangements are satisfactory.

Evaluation

None of the case study organisations had carried out any systematic analysis of the benefits of the various family-friendly working arrangements. The benefits that they described had been assessed from qualitative feedback from staff and managers.

The larger employers in the study analysed personnel data, such as absenteeism, sickness absence, turnover and numbers of full- and part-time staff by category. These were part of the standard personnel monitoring systems. These employers also carried out regular employee attitude surveys and these indicated that long hours or shift work presented problems with family life, particularly for women. Two employers had carried out a full cost assessment before introducing a particular family-friendly arrangement: one into a holiday playscheme, the other into flexitime. In both cases this had been several years ago and the data was no longer available. Three were considering whether to support a workplace nursery and were expecting that a full cost-benefit analysis would be required before a decision was made.

It appears that where family-friendly arrangements such as part-time working are introduced incrementally and in response to employee requests, each case is considered individually and the departmental manager is responsible for managing costs within his or her budget. Where the arrangement is company-wide, as in the case of flexitime, term-time shifts and childcare facilities, an initial evaluation of the costs and benefits was carried out. This is partly a matter of scale; childcare facilities are available to all staff. It also seems to relate to the formality of the arrangement. Where a few individuals negotiate to work non-standard hours, this is not widely known and is explicable as a special arrangement rather than a widespread company practice.

5 | Lessons from the case studies

◨ **There is a need to formalise flexible working practices into specific policies and criteria.**

◨ **Guidance on the practical arrangements of flexible working practices helps dispel assumptions about the difficulties of implementing such practices.**

◨ **Where practice or provision is to be provided on a significant scale, research into demand, accurate costing and evaluation will help make out a business case.**

◨ **More needs to be done to encourage the take-up of family-friendly arrangements and to reduce negative attitudes of managers and staff.**

Management of part-time and flexible work

Some clear management lessons emerge from the case studies. The majority of employers in the study were reactive and introduced family-friendly arrangements, such as part-time and flexible working, because they needed to retain the services of valued employees. Each case, they said, would be considered on its merits, depending on the requirements of the job. There is a risk that ad hoc decisions about flexible working can become inconsistent. All the case study organisations had difficulties in convincing managers of the value of flexible working. Although managers who had part-time and other flexible arrangements did not meet the difficulties that were expected, in general, information on the benefits and practicalities was not disseminated well to other managers. The latter held on to assumptions about the difficulties of managing flexibility. Most interviewees reported that they had experienced the attitude 'it can't work here' from other managers and departments. It was said that production and customer service functions were not suitable for part-time work, but the examples

in other case studies show that it can and that it is possible. These kinds of assumption may lead to requests being refused without equitable consideration and, as was reported in one case study, they could also result in part-time staff missing opportunities for promotion, without the practical possibilities being fully weighed.

It was also reported by some employees interviewed that they felt perceived as a 'problem', or asking for 'favours', when they had to negotiate to work reduced hours. A formal policy can make it easier for employees to take advantage of family-friendly arrangements and may also help reduce negative attitudes.

Some practical lessons also emerged. Lack of continuity is a bigger problem if the part-time person is employed for less than three days, but this can be reduced if the employee works daily for half a day. If the tasks of a part-time or shared job can be split into discrete areas, this also reduces continuity problems. In one example, career breaks were less successful for keeping in touch after maternity leave than providing part-time work. The latter solves the problem of 'keeping in touch' and

> **'All the case study organisations had difficulties in convincing managers of the value of flexible working.'**

is especially beneficial if business conditions and technology are changing fast.

All the case study organisations said that where employees shared a job or part-time shift, it was essential for them to have a flexible attitude. This ensured that the employer could benefit from additional cover and could adapt task allocation to fit production or customer needs.

HR managers played an important role in ensuring that requests for flexible working were dealt with consistently. They can influence managers, provide information and offer professional knowledge and advice on company policy and best practice. But the implementation of HR practice is devolved to line managers and there is a limit to how far HR can make things happen, especially if the approach to family-friendly practices is reactive. It was therefore important for family-friendly working practices to be given explicit senior management support.

According to current demographic trends and the experience of employees interviewed, there seems to be far greater scope for introducing flexible working practices. Employees who experience difficulties in balancing their work and domestic life are either out of the labour market altogether – and their skills and experience lost to employers – or working under stress at a cost to themselves and to their employer.

The lessons seem to be:

◘ Employers should positively promote family-friendly practices, with senior management support, and encourage all departments to consider the possibilities. It is important to think through the consequences of the changes, show how it would work and make out a case for it. Managers need to be aware

of the reasons for the practices and the options. Employees need to feel that they may vary their working hours or days without being perceived as a 'problem' or 'not taken seriously'. The introduction of a formal policy statement in support of family-friendly practices can be useful to give explicit recognition and focus in the company.

◘ A short statement of the reasons for introducing family-friendly arrangements and the criteria for considering flexible working will help maintain consistency and fairness. Since adaptability is a key success criterion, this should be an explicit consideration for which evidence will be sought from employees or applicants.

◘ Guidance on the practical arrangements to be considered for flexible working would help reduce assumptions about the difficulties and encourage take-up. This could include suggestions on how to divide tasks and jobs; how to ensure co-ordination and good communications between people sharing jobs and between them and their colleagues, including maintaining an employee's contacts within the company, inclusion in team briefings and staff development and training events; and, for jobs with clients and customers, detailed arrangements for cover.

◘ There may need to be explicit allocation of resources for technology, such as additional e-mail links or mobile telephones where there is a need for continuity and contact outside days in.

◘ Where part-time and flexible working arrangements are small scale, there was no reason to carry out detailed costing and evaluation. If on a larger scale, production planning and costing was necessary.

'Most family-friendly practices in the case studies have focused on the needs of women with young families. Broader questions of work–life balance were being considered by only a few, more prescient-minded employers.'

Management of time off

Paradoxically, although these are short-term and time-limited provisions, the case study organisations were more likely to have a formal policy and criteria for time off, such as parental and domestic emergencies leave. This may be because these are now requirements rather than voluntary arrangements. There were no difficulties reported, but a few commented that there was underuse of the provisions. This may be because the family-friendly approach is not yet embedded in the workplace culture, or it may be because anxieties about the cost of these provisions resulted in overestimates of likely demand.

Childcare provision

Although only one example of a holiday playscheme was included, there were some lessons that can be identified:

- There needs to be a quantifiable demand established from investigation of potential users. This could include an assessment from resignation rates after maternity leave, which may indicate numbers of staff who might have used this facility; a specific question on childcare in exit interviews; and an assessment of the numbers of staff in difficult-to-recruit or difficult-to-retain positions with young families. This will indicate whether a scheme will meets the employers' need to retain key staff, who should have priority in allocating places.

- Childcare provision works best if the facilities are adjacent to the workplace. A subsidy was also important in keeping costs down, and affordable to the categories of staff who were the main users.

Business lessons

The case studies provide evidence that there are significant advantages to employers in providing family-friendly practices. Productivity, motivation, commitment and flexibility are improved. Absenteeism and turnover are reduced, and so too are the costs of recruitment and using agencies. Although there are no calculations in the organisations in the study to establish this, all respondents said that these gains offset any additional marginal costs of providing training, support and facilities for higher numbers of staff as a result of part-time working.

Looking ahead

Most family-friendly practices in the case studies have focused on the needs of women with young families. Broader questions of work–life balance were being considered by only a few, more prescient-minded employers. Yet demographic trends suggest that employers will soon have to consider how to retain skills and recruit from alternative sources, including older people and women returners. A proportion of both categories are likely to want flexible working arrangements.

Workplace trends also show an increase in flexible working, partly as a result of market requirements for services and facilities to be available for longer hours. These case studies show that family-friendly working can benefit both the business – by retaining skills and increasing flexibility – and the employees, by enabling them to have a better work–life balance. But in order to ensure that both the business and employees' needs are met, employers need to establish objectively the scope and demand for flexibility, and create a culture that encourages the take-up of family-friendly working arrangements.

6 | Profiles of participants in the case studies

Aventis CropScience

Cambridge

Profile of the company

Aventis is a global life science company formed in 1999 from a merger of Rhône-Poulenc and Hoechst.

The company manufactures herbicides, insecticides and fungicides, and crop produce such as hybrid seeds, and has the largest research and development function in the crop science industry. It is investing significantly in bio-technology, which is predicted to become the main new process in crop protection.

The company consists of Aventis Pharma and Aventis Agriculture, of which Aventis CropScience is a major business, with 15.8 per cent of the global crop science market. The head office of the parent company is in Strasbourg, France, and the company locations include the USA, Brazil, France, Belgium, Germany, the UK and Japan.

In the UK, Aventis CropScience UK has manufacturing sites in Norwich, Hauxton, Cambridge and a smaller one in Widnes, and a research and development function in Ongar, Essex. The case study focused on Cambridge.

Human resources

Aventis CropScience is not a major employer of part-time staff. There are 1,373 full-time and 25 part-time employees, with a high level of professional staff, particularly in research and development, and 286 women employees. It focuses on seven key values, the first of which is 'Respect for People', and includes 'Valuing individuality' and 'Balance between work and home life.'

The main work–life balance practices are part-time and flexitime working, and career breaks. The main reason for introducing career breaks was to retain qualified professional women staff, especially highly experience and skilled research staff. Paid and unpaid leave are available for a range of domestic reasons and days off can also be accumulated under flexitime arrangements. The company offers extended maternity leave. The flexitime scheme is well established, but not at all sites, and was introduced in 1974. Since the merger, the company is assessing its practices and considering whether to extend flexitime to all sites.

Workplace change

In addition to the merger, which affected the location of staff and work, the company has experienced significant changes due to technological developments and new research, both of which are critical for the company. The company is not considering extending its work–life balance practices, except for flexitime to sites where there is no scheme.

British Sugar

Peterborough

Profile of the company

British Sugar is the UK's leading supplier of sugar and sugar products to the food and drink manufacturing industry, catering and retail markets, the latter under the 'Silver Spoon' brand. The company employs about 1,450 people, of whom 189 are women, at its factories located in the east of England, the West Midlands, and the head office in Peterborough. In addition, the company employs a further 600 seasonal employees each winter for processing beet, of which last year there were 91 women. Apart from seasonal employees, the company does not rely heavily on non-standard types of employment contract. The company recognises unions, namely the GMB, TGWU and AEEU, negotiates pay and holds regular consultations with union representatives.

Human resources

The company has a progressive HR strategy that focuses on the company–employee relationship, how employees are managed, leadership styles and values – to achieve the right culture to deliver the business strategy. The approach is to involve employees, value their contribution and offer good pay and conditions. This approach is reflected in the British Sugar family-friendly guidelines, which state that the company is going beyond the minimum required by law in order to demonstrate a real commitment to developing good employment practices, enhance its position as a blue-chip company and increase its ability to attract and retain high-calibre employees into the future. The guidelines were preceded by consultations with staff, such as women returning from maternity leave, and were introduced partly in response to comments made in an employee opinion survey. The guidelines were introduced to business areas through informal discussions and presentations by HR managers.

The company offers part-time work and job share, and home-working in some areas. Domestic and paternity leave provisions have been improved because of recent legal changes. The company offers enhanced maternity pay, and flexible working hours prior to maternity leave and on return from leave. Even before the changes in legislation the company encouraged managers to adopt a sympathetic approach to employees with personal difficulties and, where appropriate, allowed paid leave to be taken.

Workplace change

The main changes in the company in the last five years have been structural, including reorganisation of the board and group, and of individual departments following a business review.

Bidwells

Cambridge

Profile of the company

Bidwells is a property consultancy, a partnership of 326 partners and employees, 46 per cent of whom are women. Two-thirds of employees are professionally qualified staff. The firm has 50 part-time staff, including four men, and 15 self-employed contractors. The head office is in Cambridge, and there are also offices in Bury St Edmunds, Ipswich, London, Northampton, Norwich and two in Scotland.

The firm deals with the buying, selling and renting of domestic and commercial property and land, and, in Scotland, deals with ecological advice, estate, forest and moorland management.

Human resources

The HR policy is based on a high level of concern about what is right for people. The firm provides part-time and a little seasonal working for work experience, some home-working and has self-employed consultants. It offers paid parental leave, domestic and study leave, and extended maternity pay. Extended leave is also possible. The main reason for flexible working arrangements is the need to retain qualified trained staff, especially women. The company is built on the skills of its professional staff and there is a high degree of individual judgement and expertise in the job, which it cannot afford to lose. The need to retain valuable experience and skills is also leading the firm to consider the implications of employing semi-retired professional staff as self-employed consultants.

Workplace change

Developments in information technology have affected working practices most in the last five years, and have made it possible for staff to work from home informally, but there are still questions about access to data, which limits the scope for working away from the office.

Gilchris

Fakenham

Profile of the company

Gilchris is a privately owned company that manufactures chocolates, petits fours and novelty confectionery for the retail industry. There are 499 employees, mostly working in production, 264 of whom are women. The company works a variety of shifts, including evening, early morning, weekend and term-time shifts, the last known as the school shift. The main production peak is from August to Easter, in preparation for Halloween, Christmas and Easter itself.

Human resources

Because of the fluctuations in production, flexibility is built into the working arrangements and holiday entitlements. The variety of shifts gives scope for part-time working. The company is looking at the possibility of a type of annualised hours contract to avoid reliance on temporary staff at busy times. The company also offers a flexible holiday scheme under which employees who work on Saturdays in peak periods gain extra days' holiday to take in the low season. There is some limited informal working at home. Paternity leave can be taken from 'floating' annual leave entitlement and extended leave is possible at managers' discretion.

The company employs many mothers, and also both parents, of young children, and is keen to help staff with families to balance their work and lives. The company provides information about childcare and nursery facilities in the area. The term-time shift is popular, especially with women returning from maternity leave. School shift staff tend to be settled and reliable and have a lot in common with each other. The company is flexible about allowing days off for additional school holidays and training days. They take the initiative in finding out the dates of school holidays and extra days off from Norfolk Education Authority, and circulate the dates to staff on the school shift.

The company has good links with the local Jobcentre. Before the school shift was introduced, it held an open day to explain what was being offered and received much interest from local people.

Workplace change

The company has experienced many changes in the last five years as it has grown and introduced new machinery to increase output. Working times and arrangements have changed along with the location and organisation of work.

Johnson Matthey

Royston

Profile of the company

The Johnson Matthey Group is a global corporation, with a head office in London and its main subsidiaries in several European countries, the USA, Canada, Japan, Hong Kong and Singapore. The group produces and refines precious metals, such as platinum, gold and silver; manufactures catalysts and other related chemicals for the automobile industry; pharmaceutical ingredients; and manufactures colours and coatings for the glass, ceramics and tableware industries.

Johnson Matthey Royston incorporates employees from all divisions of the group. There are 811 employees at the site, the majority (637) of whom are full-time males, employed mainly in manufacturing and technical departments.

Human resources

The company has a strong commitment to training and development and to providing a good working environment.

In production, the typical pattern is shift working. The company operates part-time working in some areas and has started job sharing. There is a range of flexible leave arrangements, general maternity benefits, sabbaticals after 25 years' service, up to four weeks' unpaid parental leave per annum, up to five days' domestic leave and discretionary leave for other purposes. Maternity, parental and domestic leave arrangements were revised in the light of current legislation and the company is extending part-time and other flexible working on a case-by-case basis, mainly where there is a need to offer flexibility to retain a key employee's skills and experience.

Workplace change

The company faces continuous market-led changes in technology, which results in changes in the organisation of work and working times, and it introduced continuous 24-hour working several years ago.

Leathes Prior

Norwich

Profile of the company

Leathes Prior is a firm of solicitors located in the centre of Norwich. There are 12 partners and 58 employees, with nine part-time staff.

Human resources

The firm operates part-time working, flexible hours, job share and informal home-working. There is also a part-time consultant who is a semi-retired employee. The firm offers extended and unpaid leave for domestic and paternity purposes and other contingencies.

The firm introduced part-time working mainly in order to retain the skills and experience of legal and hard-to-recruit staff, and found that because part-time work was available, several women returned after maternity leave who might otherwise have left. Because part-time working has been successful, it has been extended across all areas of work. IT and voicemail facilities permit home-working for senior staff.

Leo Electron Microscopy Ltd

Cambridge

Profile of the company

Leo Electron Microscopy is a high-technology international company and world leader in the design and manufacture of both scanning and transmission electron microscopes. Its instruments are used in a variety of applications, ranging from research by leading scientists in semiconductors, materials or life sciences, to industrial quality control, inspection and failure analysis.

The company employs 350 staff in total, 84 of whom are based in Cambridge. A high proportion of staff are highly qualified and possess specialised technical skills. There are 12 women employed on the Cambridge site.

Human resources

The HR approach is based on an open, flexible company culture where employees are respected and trusted, and most working practices are informal. There are by necessity company policies to comply with legislative requirements, set standards and provide a consistent approach. The work ethic is not to work long hours, but to use working time effectively and productively. The company operates limited home-working, subject to approval in advance by senior management. Take-up of part-time working is small. Annual leave is treated flexibly, depending on operational cover within the section or department. Staff can take three days' paternity leave. There is provision for domestic leave, which, combined with informal flexitime, allows staff to attend to domestic matters.

Workplace change

Leo Cambridge has been through major restructuring within the last two years. As an international company exporting throughout the world, it is affected by market forces and technological developments. Leo's approach to computing technology is to use the latest techniques and products to enhance the ease of use and interoperability of its products to maintain its status as a world leader. This affects the organisation of work, working arrangements, and has meant that some areas of work have been outsourced.

Norfolk Mental Health Care NHS Trust

Norwich

Profile of the organisation

Norfolk Mental Health Care NHS Trust provides mental health care in a range of community and in-patient settings. It has 1,688 employees, a large majority of whom (over 1,100) are nursing, medical staff and psychologists, and a further 124 are paramedical staff, such as occupational therapists and physiotherapists. Women make up 70 per cent of staff, and almost one-third of staff are part time. Additionally, there are over 350 'bank' or self-employed temporary staff.

Human resources

The contractual terms and conditions of staff, including maternity leave and maternity pay entitlement, are decided by the NHS Whitley Council (the joint NHS negotiating body), and apply to employment in any health authority. For more general employment policies for which the precise details are not centrally decided, such as family-friendly arrangements and equal opportunities, the Whitley Council will issue guidance.

The necessity for 24-hour shift work and the high proportion of women employed means that work–life balance and childcare are major concerns for staff; this has been confirmed in staff surveys. In relation to family-friendly policies, Norfolk Mental Health Trust has its own job-share scheme and guidelines on family and domestic leave, and maternity leave and pay. The guidelines on job share make it clear that the trust wishes to encourage and promote the practice and include practical information about how to apply for the arrangement. A job-share register is maintained in the HR department, comprising people who wish to work on this basis in the trust. There is also a remote-working pilot, and people working a compressed work week.

Norfolk and Norwich Health Care NHS Trust

Norwich

Profile of the organisation

Norfolk and Norwich is an NHS hospital with about 4,500 employees. Nursing and medical staff represent over 50 per cent of the total staffing, with a high proportion of women and also 'bank' staff.

Human resources

Like the Norfolk Mental Health Care NHS Trust, the contractual terms and conditions of staff, including maternity leave and maternity pay entitlement, are mainly decided by the NHS General Whitley Council (the joint NHS negotiating body), and apply to employment in any health authority.

Although the main focus in this case study was on childcare provision, the trust is also reviewing its flexible working arrangements and recently issued a discussion document to encourage departments to provide a greater choice of working arrangements to staff and allow a more flexible approach.

The trust has had a holiday playscheme for about 20 years. Initially this was for the summer holidays, and for the past 10 years has extended to all school holidays, apart from Christmas and spring half-term. The current scheme takes 40 children and is open to all staff on a first-come basis, although in practice it is used mainly by nursing, administrative and clerical staff. The administration of the scheme is done internally by two staff in the HR department. Application forms are circulated a month before the scheme begins with a deadline for booking a place. If there are spare places, they are offered to staff in other NHS trusts in the area. Staff can book single days or part days, a week and extra sessions.

The scheme is run in the premises of a nearby local school, and is staffed by a play leader, deputy and three assistants, and sometimes additional volunteers. The cost is £9.00 per day and the scheme is subsidised by about £6,000 per year by the trust, and also by the Friends of the Hospital and the sports and social club.

Rebus Software Ltd

Peterborough

Profile of the company

Rebus is a global software company specialising in developing software and providing online support for human resource and payroll information systems. The company has subsidiaries and distribution centres in the USA, Australia, New Zealand, Hong Kong, Singapore, France and the Netherlands.

Human resources

The company employs part-time staff and, in order to provide extended hours for customer services, there is a bank of part-time and seasonal temporary staff. A partial flexitime system is in operation, with core hours from 10.00am to 4.00pm, and staff on the help desk work in early and late shifts. The company offers a range of leave, including paternity, domestic, compassionate, study and unpaid leave. Extended leave of up to five days is available.

Workplace change

The main change affecting the company in the last five years is its continued expansion, both in the establishment of new subsidiaries and in the provision of extended customer services. This has affected both the time of day and the hours worked, leading to the introduction of flexitime and shift work.

Ridgeons

Cambridge

Profile of the company

The Ridgeon Group is a privately owned family business with 17 branches supplying building materials throughout East Anglia. It employs 665 people: 536 men and 129 women. The majority of employees have customer contact, face-to-face or by telephone.

Human resources

Ridgeons is a family business and its owners have encouraged a company culture that supports family life. The group philosophy statement includes 'mutual respect' and 'foster a thoughtful, caring and helpful attitude towards others' among its values. In response to customer demand for extended opening hours, the company offers a variety of working hours and flexible times, including part-time work and job share, and seasonal work such as vacation employment of students. There are currently 21 men and 72 women working part time. The company also has a positive attitude towards older employees. For example, the company recently targeted recruitment at people aged over 55 years and employed a 72-year-old in security. There is a range of discretionary paid leave arrangements and also parental and domestic leave.

Workplace change

The biggest change in the group in the last five years has been the recent acquisition of nine new branches, which doubled its number of branches and extended its locations further into Essex, Suffolk and Norfolk. This resulted in organisational changes and increased demand for internal support such as training. Another change in the last five years has been the extension of trading hours, to all day Saturday in one Cambridge Branch.

References

BAILYN L. (1993)

Breaking the Mold: Women, men and time in the new corporate world. Tampa, Florida, Free Press.

BEVAN S., DENCH S., TAMKIN P. and CUMMINGS J. (1999)

Family-Friendly Employment: The business case. DfEE Research report RR 136. London, DfEE.

CASEY B., METCALF N. and MILLWARD N. (1997)

Employers' Use of Flexible Labour. London, Policy Studies Institute.

COOPER C. and WORRAL L. (1998)

The Quality of Work–life Survey: A survey of managers. University of Manchester Institute of Science and Technology.

CULLY M., WOODLAND S., O'REILLY A. and DIX G. (1999)

Britain at Work. London, Routledge.

CURRAN J., KITCHING J., ABBOT B. and MILLS V. (1993)

Employment and Employment Relations in the Small Service Sector Enterprise – A report. ESRC Centre for Research on Small Service Sector Enterprises. Kingston, Kingston University Business School.

DALY K. J. (1996)

Families and Time: Keeping pace in a hurried culture. London, Sage Publications.

DEPARTMENT FOR EDUCATION AND EMPLOYMENT. (2000)

Work–Life Balance: Changing patterns in a changing world. London, DfEE.

DEX S. and MCCULLOCH A. (1995)

Flexible Employment in Britain: A statistical analysis. Manchester, Equal Opportunities Commission. Discussion series no. 15.

DEX S. and SCHEIBL F. (1998)

'Is there a business case for firms to have family-friendly policies?' Judge Institute Working Paper. Cambridge, University of Cambridge.

DEX S., SCHEIBL F., SMITH C. and COUSSEY M. (2000)

New Working Patterns. London, The Centre for Tomorrow's Company.

FORTH J., LISSENBURGH S., CALLENDER C. and MILLWARD N. (1997)

Family-Friendly Working Arrangements in Britain, 1996. London, Department for Education and Employment. Research Report No. 16.

GUEST D. and CONWAY N. (1998)

Fairness at Work and the Psychological Contract. London, Institute of Personnel and Development.

HEYES J. (1997)

'Annualised hours and the "knock": the organisation of working time in a chemicals plant'. *Work Employment and Society*. Vol. 11, No. 1. pp65–81.

HOLTERMAN S. (1995)

'The costs and benefits to British employers of measures to promote equal opportunity'. *Gender Work and Organisations*. Vol. 2, No. 3.

INSTITUTE OF PERSONNEL AND DEVELOPMENT. (1999)

Living to Work? London, IPD.

LEWIS S. and LEWIS J. (1996)

The Work-Family Challenge: Rethinking employment. London, Sage Publications.

NEW WAYS TO WORK. (1993)

Change at the Top: Working flexibly at senior and managerial levels. London, New Ways to Work.

PURCELL K. (1997)

'The implications of employment flexibility for equal opportunities'. Paper for British Universities Industrial Relations Association Annual Conference, University of Bath, 4–6 July 1999.

SCHEIBL F. and DEX S. (1998)

'Should we have more family-friendly policies?' *European Management Journal*. Vol. 16, No. 5.

THATCHER M. (1996)

'Family favourites' *People Manangement*. Vol. 2, No. 20.

TRADES UNION CONGRESS. (1995)

The Pros and Cons of Part-Time Working: A TUC survey. London, Trades Union Congress.

WILKINSON H., RADLEY S., CHRISTIE I., LAWSON G. and SAINSBURY J. (1997)

Time Out: The costs and benefits of paid parental leave. London, Demos.